SO, YOU WANT TO BE IN SALES?

Ten Things I Wish I Knew Before Starting In Sales

Bo Hamrick

So, You Want To Be In Sales?

Cover designed by Bo Hamrick

Bo Hamrick
Visit my website at www.bohamrick.com

Printed in the United States of America

First Printing: April 2018
Create Space Publishing

ISBN-13: 9781717102430

ISBN-10: 1717102433

This book is dedicated to my wife. Convincing you to go on a date with me and ultimately to marry me was my best sale ever.

To Emma, Hannah, & Carter: You are the reason I work and my motivation to make the world a better place.

CONTENTS

INTRODUCTION

The harder the conflict, the more glorious
the triumph.
—Thomas Paine

S ALES IS A DIFFICULT PROFESSION. It doesn't matter if you are in the Business - to - Business (B2B), Business – to - Consumer (B2C), or Business – to - Government (B2G) sales environment, each one is hard. Each market, each job, and each product bring its own set of challenges. Go look on Amazon at all the books available for sale on "sales." My search produced 1,376,953 results for books about "sales." You can now add this book to the list. When I go look for all the conferences, blogs, podcasts, websites and gurus for sales professionals to spend their money on, one of two thoughts come to my mind: First, sales professionals must make a ton of money and like to spend their money on books, conferences, blogs, podcasts, websites, and gurus! Or second, sales professionals are starved for information and not just information but the right information. In this short book, you will learn what ten things I wish I knew before starting in sales. In addition, I have included a chapter on financial planning for sales professionals and a reference chapter for suggestions on podcasts, books, apps, and tools that you may find useful.

In this book, you will find ten tips or pieces of advice that should help you stimulate your thought process around being a better sales professional. In addition to the ten things I wish I knew before getting into sales, I have included a bonus tip around your financial wellbeing and a final chapter on sales resources. These are books, podcasts, and apps that I find to make my life a bit easier as a salesperson. These ten tips have been cultivated over 15 plus years, carrying a bag for multiple companies. I have sold consumer products like power tools, financial and insurance products, business services, medical equipment and enterprise level computer software. Regardless of the product sold, the territory, or any other variable you could imagine, the ten tips have stood the test of time.

Why should you read this book? That is a great question. If you are just getting started in sales, if you are thinking about changing careers into the sales profession, or maybe you are thinking about starting a business and initially you will also be doing the sales. Or maybe if your sales career has grown stagnant or you are not experiencing the results you were hoping for. If so, this book will give you some tips, tricks, guidelines and examples of ways you could become a better sales professional. This book is not going to give you scripts to read, or sales processes to follow, or make any promises that you will be successful. But what will be delivered is a book that can give you insight into the sales profession that you would only normally gain with experience. Take my experience and learn from it. Take my mistakes and my errors and learn from them and speed up your time to becoming a top performing sales professional.

I appreciate you taking the time to read this book. As you are reading, and begin developing questions, please feel free to reach out to me on Twitter at www.twitter.com/bohamrick. You can also connect with me on LinkedIn at www.linkedin.com/in/bohamrick. In your request to connect please let me know that you are reading the book. You can also find other posts from me on my website at www.bohamrick.com.

After you have finished the book, I would be appreciative of your honest feedback on the book on www.amazon.com.

NOBODY CARES ABOUT YOU

Nobody cares how much you know, until
they know how much you care.
—Theodore Roosevelt

I KNOW THIS MAY SOUND harsh, but, nobody cares about you! I say this not to imply that you are worthless or that your prospects and customers are mean and heartless individuals for not caring about you. But nobody cares about you! In fact, this rule is not even about you. It is all about how you deliver your message. This is about how you present your value to your prospects and customers.

Let me tell you about a company, Acme (not the real company name) that works with some of my clients. This company is a great company; they have a great product and my clients that use their software are all happy. However, they almost always shoot themselves in the foot at the beginning of every sales presentation. When they give a presentation to my clients, during the first 30 minutes of the sales presentation, they will talk about how great they are, how many clients they have, how much venture capital money they have raised, the awards they have won and even how great their corporate headquarters is. The list goes on and on. I have watched my clients as they roll their eyes, check the time on their smartphones and completely zone out of the presentation. They do not care about how great this company is. They want to know how great the company's products or services are going to make them!

This company does still win many deals, but most of the deals they lose are because the prospect is turned off by this initial presentation. What is wrong with their presentation? The focus is on them. They focus on what matters to them. They are using me, us, and we pronouns throughout the presentation.

So, if I am not supposed to talk about how great I am, what am I supposed to talk about?

Every time a prospect or a customer attends a sales presentation or even watches an ad on TV, their mind is subconsciously trying to answer one simple question. In fact, as you read this book, your mind is also subconsciously trying to answer the same simple question.

The question is: WIIFM

What is WIIFM? It is not W.I.I.F.M., Home for all your favorite hits on the radio! (read this in your best Radio DJ

Voice). WIIFM stands for What's In It For Me. This is the question your prospects and clients are asking. If I use your product – What's In It For Me? If I buy your car – What's In It For Me? If I purchase your financial product – What's In It For Me? If I buy this house from you – What's In It For Me? You need to be able to answer that question during your sales pitch. I don't care if you are doing door – to – door sales, selling a car, selling a house, or some complex business software. Everyone's the same...What's In It For Me? Business – to – Business sales...What's In It For Me? Business – to – Consumer sales...What's In It For Me? Business – to – Government sales...What's In It For Me?

If you can answer that question for your customers and prospects, they can start to see how the use of your product or service will benefit them. This will also make you more likeable. We will talk about why that is important later in the book.

To improve on this skill with your sales presentations, I challenge you to record your phone calls, sales pitches, and conversations with your clients and prospects. Look over your proposals, emails and presentations. Are you using me, we, I, and us, or are you using **them** and **you,** or if you are in the south like me: **Y'all.** Initially it will be difficult to change the way you talk, especially if your organization's marketing and sales material have a "me" focus instead of a **them** focus. If you are like most sales professionals, you are not the person designing the marketing material. You will not have much control over them, but you have control over how much you use them.

In addition to looking at the pronouns that you use, how are you describing the features of the product? Take my car for example. I have a Toyota Highlander. One of the features of the vehicle is LDS or Lane Departure System. I get an annoying beep every time I cross over a lane without my turn signal on. That is the feature. But What's In It For Me? My dealer shouldn't be talking about the annoying beep, that's a feature. They need to be telling me about how it can alert you of danger if you are distracted by technology or because you are tired. This is the benefit of the feature. This is the part that is in it for Me. They could further strengthen their case by sharing a story with me. Do they know of a customer who was driving home late one night from work and fell asleep at the wheel and was awoken by the annoying beep? Maybe they can add some insight. In his book, *Insight Selling*, Michael Harris says, "When Insight Sellers deliver insights they shock customers by breaking the customers' thought patterns with one that is new and improved."[1] Going back to my car example, when the dealer tells me the beep will save me from distracted driving or diving while tired, he could back this up with some insight and state a fact about the percent of time the average driver, drives distracted. For example 64% of all road accidents in the United States have a cell phone involved in them.[2]

Why are insights so valuable? At first when that car salesperson is telling me about the annoying beep and how it will save me from distracted driving, I am internally saying

---

[1] See recommended books in the last chapter.
[2] www.distracteddriveraccidents.com/25-shokcing-distracted-driving-statistics

to myself, "Self...Not you, you never drive distracted and if you did, you are really good at it." Then when they provide the statistic of 64% of all accidents involve a cell phone, now I get honest with myself and wonder how good of a driver am I really?

These insights will challenge me to see the value of the annoying beep. I start to see the feature as a benefit that I want to purchase.

Benefits can be valued in a number of different ways. For starters, benefits can be monetary. For example, paying bills online can save me the cost of the stamp for every bill I pay. This is a hard savings that I can truly account for.

The second way a product can provide you benefits is with a time savings. For example, checking into my flight on the app, saves me from standing in line at the airport. At a busy airport, that could save me 30 minutes or more per trip. Thirty minutes of savings could mean I get to sleep in later or see another customer before going to the airport. All of these are benefits of time for me.

The final way that people see a benefit is prestige or status. You see this in luxury brands; having a Rolex makes you feel as if you have arrived. A Rolex tells time just like any watch would. Having a Rolex does not make you a better time manager. The only benefit to having a Rolex is the feeling of status or prestige. For many people, that is all they need!

By focusing your message on how it helps your audience will allow you to answer the important question of your prospects and clients: What's In It For Me?

Are you new to your company? Are you lacking good insightful stories to share with customers and prospects? That's okay. You are not alone. Most marketing companies are not aware of these types of stories either. The best way to find these stories is to talk with your existing clients. Ask one of the senior sales professionals to introduce you to one of their clients and ask them what life was like before they started using your company's product. Since using your company's product, what has changed? How have things gotten better for them? Are there any cost savings they have attributed to the use of your product or service? Are there any time savings they have seen because of the use of your product or service? Finding these stories is like finding gold. You can use these stories over and over again in your sales process and since they are real life examples, your clients and prospects will be able to answer the question: What's In It For Me?

AVOID THE SALES ROLLER COASTER

Don't watch the clock, do what it does.
Keep Going!
—Sam Levenson

MY WIFE AND I ALMOST never made it to the alter. We were still dating each other, and I was in Virginia spending a summer weekend with her and her family. They wanted to go to Busch Gardens. We go into the park and Leslie says she wants to ride a roller coaster. I tell her I am not a big fan of roller coasters, but she tells me this one is not that bad. Let's face it, I was a college guy still trying to impress this beautiful woman I was dating. We get on Apollo's Chariot, and Leslie's reason for it not being that bad was because it does not go upside down. The ride begins with an initial ascent. My nerves are shot, my knuckles are white as my hands clamp onto the safety handles and up we go. As we get toward the top of the first hill the coaster starts to slow down, and you can hear the click, click, click up the hill and then over the apex we go and down over 210 feet at 73 miles per hour...hurling our helpless bodies toward the ground. At that point my face turns as white as snow and then, according to my wife, as green as The Grinch. I had an overwhelming sense of fear and anger written all over my face. Leslie recalls now that she seriously thought I was going to break up with her either on the ride or as soon as we got back on solid ground. It did cross my mind. I do not like roller coasters, never have, never will.

What is it that scares me about roller coasters? One word. Control. I do not like sitting there in the seat with no control over how slowly we climb the hill, how fast we go down the hill and if something goes wrong, I have no way of preventing it.

Many sales professionals spend their entire career on a sales roller coaster.

What is the sales roller coaster? Well, it could be several things. First, you finish a quarter with a strong push, offering discounts and incentives so that you can hit and exceed your personal quota. Your company does everything they can to help you achieve that goal. Then a new quarter starts, and your pipeline is dry. You spend the rest of the beginning of the new quarter filling up your funnel, only to empty it again at the end of the next quarter. As opposed to having a steady stream of deals rolling through your pipeline throughout the year, quarter, month or week. For many sales professionals and for most companies, this happens all the time and most people are resigned to the fact of "that's just how it is." Or, "that is how we have always done it." You can probably feel that you are on a sales roller coaster. But if you cannot tell if you are, you can look at your daily or weekly activity. You will see that you start out strong, calling a certain number of people per day, setting appointments, and taking customer service calls, etc. Then your call activity starts to drop off. Your sales eventually start to drop off and then you are back to focusing on your call numbers again.

Another sales roller coaster that you could ride on would be your motivation level or excitement level. Close a big deal? – Happiness through the roof. Lose a big deal? – Depressed beyond belief. Another common sales roller coaster for your emotions is when you are cold calling and trying to set appointments. You get a few "yes" responses in a row and you start to feel good about your ability, then you get on a long streak of no responses and your feelings slide into the negative world.

Regardless of the roller coaster you are riding, a good sales professional finds a way to level out the curves or flatten the hills so that their activity, sales, and sanity all stay at an even keel.

So, let's take a look at managing the mental side of the roller coaster. As I mentioned at the opening of the book, sales is a difficult profession. There is no greater high than making a sale, but in order to get to the sale you must go through a difficult journey. I am going to talk about activity here shortly and in my example, we will discuss an instance of cold calling 200 people. By calling those 200 people, you would get on average two people to say yes. That means that you are successful just one percent of the time. That also means that 198 people told you no. Being told no is a tough thing to get used to. You must put it into the concept of a game. Later in the book we will talk about how being uncomfortable is normal. Being told no 198 times is uncomfortable. But if you can realize that it is all part of the process to get you to the two yesses you need, the 198 do not seem that bad.

Gaming the sales system is the best way to manage your emotions in sales. Imagine if I told you that I would pay $1.00 for every mile that you run. Every day you go out and run two miles and at the end of the week, I will give you $14.00 (2 miles a day x 7 days = 14 miles). It is very easy for you to manage your expectations and your effort level because you know every mile you run is going to earn you a dollar.

But what if I told you that you had to run two miles a day for seven days and that some of your miles will earn you nothing, and some miles will earn you $7.00. The first day on the first mile you earn a $7.00 mile. You are most likely excited and will keep running, but the next few miles that you run earn you nothing! On the last day of the week, you have gone 5 straight runs without making a dollar. You will start to get discouraged; you will start to think that the payment is never going to come. But you go out there on the last day and run and earn that $7.00.

In both examples, you run 14 miles and earn $14.00. In both scenarios you were paid the same for your efforts. But in one example you knew that every mile you ran was going to produce $1.00 and in the other example you had no idea which mile was going to produce the $7.00 for you.

I am sure you can guess which of the running examples is like sales. You need to do the activities required of your job each day, but you have no idea which phone call, which demo, which sales opportunity may produce the sale this week. All that you can control is your activity. A lot of sales organizations are going to talk with you about "dialing for dollars." The premise behind dialing for dollars is the same as paying you $1.00 for every run. Every time you pick up the phone, make a cold call, or interact with a client – You need to view it as if you are getting paid $1.00. No, you are not actually getting paid for your activity but you have to realize that every activity that you perform gets you one step closer to your goals of making a sale.

Aside from dialing for dollars, another approach you can take to keep your emotions in check is to do the things you hate at the right time. I was in an interview a few years back and the hiring manager asked me a question that he stated, had no right or wrong answer. The question was when is the right time to cold call? I told him the right time to cold call is right after I make a sale. The hiring manager was stunned and said that while there is not a right or wrong answer to this question, my answer was the best he had ever heard. He then asked me why I think cold calling after a sale is the best time to cold call. I told him that after I make a sale, I am as high as I can get with my job. I am excited about my job and the upcoming commission; I am confident in my abilities as a sales professional, and I am confident in my company's ability to meet the needs of my prospects. So, you should harness that excitement and go make a cold call.

My thought process for this can be used for a number of things. There are numerous studies that show in the morning is when you are the most creative and driven to get your work completed. Knowing that information and assuming it holds true for you, you should focus some of your least favorite tasks for during that time frame in the morning. Hate cold calling? Go ahead and get it over with while you are fresh and engaged in your day. Do you love cold calling? Save it for the end of the day. Your energy level will be down; your excitement level will be down, but your love for the task will carry you through the activity.

A hot buzz word in pop-culture is "hacking." Life hacking refers to any trick, shortcut, skill or novelty method that increases productivity and efficiency. You need to find ways to hack your sales activities. Doing the hard or unpleasant task when you are the most fresh and ready to attack the day or right after a sale when your mental state is positive is one of many hacks you can employ to help you in your career.

The other sales roller coaster we discussed is the sales activity and sales roller coaster that happens each month, quarter, and year. Let me tell you a story about a colleague of mine. We will call him John. I had just started with this company and I was talking with John, who was one of the senior sales reps. I asked John how his week was going, and he said, "This week is kind of slow." "Why?" I asked. He continued, "Well last week I had a couple of big presentations and it took a lot of my time performing them and getting prepared, so I did not make many calls last week." This type of experience happens often for sales professionals.

In order to avoid the sales roller coaster, you need to know a few things. First, what are the key activities in your sales process and the client's buying process? The buying process is huge, remember...No one cares about you. After you know what activities you need to do, how many of those activities do you need to do to close a sale? What is your average sales size? How many sales must you close to get to your quota?

Below is a very simplified example of what I am talking about. For this sales person, his quota was $10,400. He averages $100.00 per sale, meaning he needs to close 104 sales for the year. Based on a 52-week year, he needs to make two sales per week. The company has done some research and is confident that the average sales rep in its company makes about 200 phone calls to make two sales. So, for this sales professional, I would look at this matrix:

Dials	Meetings	Demo	Negotiate	Sales	Avg $ / Sale
200	20	10	5	2	$100.00

Based on the above example, if I make 200 phone calls, I will average 20 introductory meetings. If I am able to have 20 meetings, I will get ten opportunities to demonstrate my company's abilities. If I get ten demonstrations, roughly half will start some form of negotiation with me. If I can get five to negotiate, I am able to close two deals with an average sale of $100.00 each. Two sales of $100.00 each gives me $200.00 in sales per week and should net out to $10,400 at the end of the year.

A bit of caution about my example: first, it is very simplistic. Second, it talks in averages. Your very first week on a new job or in a new territory, you are not going to have 20 meetings set up for you. You also are most likely not going to make two sales that very first week. Likewise, you will have weeks that you make three or four sales, or your average sales is below or above the $100.00 average. But typically, at the end of the year, the averages will start to prove themselves correct.

Another thing to keep in mind with this is your time to close or the length of your sales cycle. Again, let's imagine you are new rep and have just been assigned your territory. The first couple of weeks will require some ramp up. See below:

Week	Dials	Meetings	Demo	Negotiate	Sales	Avg$/Sale
1	200	10	5	2	1	$100
2	200	20	9	4	2	$90
3	200	20	10	5	1	$120
4	200	20	10	5	2	$100

The first week shows the ramp up time needed to turn these dials into meetings and demos. The longer your sales cycle is, the longer the ramp up time. I would advise you during those first few weeks that if you do not have enough meetings on the calendar or find yourself with empty time slots on your calendar to make more calls. Also, if you ever look a week or two out and the schedule is not already full, you need to make more calls to make sure you can fill up your week.

The above example is an overly simplistic example. There can be more complicated plans. For myself, I track the following activities:

- Lead email (200 per week)
- Phone Calls (10 per week)
- Introductory meetings (8 per week)
- Discovery meetings (3 per week)
- Evaluation plan meetings (3 per week)
- Demonstrations (2 per week)
- New opportunities created (3 per week)
- New opportunity dollars created ($29,166.67 per week)
- Sales (1 per week)
- Sales Dollars ($7,291.67 per week)

In addition to the above activities that I track, each of my opportunities is tracked to make sure all the following activities are completed:

- Key clients contacts identified
- Scheduled discovery call
- Initial qualifications met
- Discovery call completed
- Client timeline identified
- Power sponsor Id'ed
- Demo completed
- Migration plan developed
- Proposal generated
- Return on Investment developed
- Scoping call completed
- Verbal approval obtained
- Contract delivered

- Contract terms approved
- Closed

As you can see, there are a ton of steps to make my sales process and a ton of tasks that must be completed. This example is by no means the most difficult I have seen but it is detailed. By following these steps, it allows me to stay on track with my opportunities.

If you need any assistance with building out your activity tracker or the steps needed in your sales process, you should first work with your manager to get this developed and then run everything by your mentor. Finally, if you are interested in individualized coaching, setting up your activity tracker or steps in your sales process, I am available to assist you. I have a sample activity tracker on my website (www.bohamrick.com). If you feel you need a more personalized tracker or your company would like some consulting assistance to help develop this, you can reach out to me on Twitter (www.twitter.com/Bohamrick), LinkedIn (www.linkedin.com/in/bohamrick), or on my website (www.bohamrick.com).

EVERY DAY IS AN INTERVIEW

*Become the person who would attract the
results you seek.*
—Jim Cathcart

WHAT DO YOU TYPICALLY WEAR when you go in for your first interview? Most likely you wear a suit. For men, you will wear a suit with a button-down shirt and a tie. For ladies, a suit with a blouse is appropriate. You should be wearing a dark blue or charcoal suit with a white shirt and a conservative tie or a scarf, for the ladies. Most likely you all know this already. Now the important question: Why? Why do you dress that way for an interview? For many of you, the answer may be, "because I was told to." For the rest of you, it is because you want to put your best foot forward. I have heard of situations where a company may tell the interviewee to wear business casual attire, and if so, that is fine, but I recommend you always wear a suit. The main point of this chapter, however, is not to talk about how to dress for an interview, but for you to treat every day like an interview. In short, always dress to impress your audience. Every company that you work for will have different dress codes. But you will have three dress codes to follow.

The first is the company dress code. Your company may have a uniform or a standard for how you should dress when in the office or when in front of clients. You should view your company dress code as the bare minimum. For example, my current company requires me in a suit for business meetings with clients. They prefer a tie, but it is optional. I have had many different dress codes throughout my career. When I worked for Black and Decker, I wore khaki pants and a company logo polo or button down. When I worked for Ferguson, it was dress slacks with a shirt and tie. At AXA Advisors, my dress code was a suit and tie. When I worked at Cintas, I had two different dress codes. If I were on a route with a driver, I was in a Cintas Uniform, and if I was on sales calls, I wore a suit and tie. When I went to work for Verathon Medical, I wore a suit and tie.

The second code to follow is the customer dress code. Let me give you an example of when this might matter. As I said, my current company's dress code was to wear a suit and dress shirt, and a tie was optional when meeting clients. I was dressed for some of my first meetings with these clients. I included the tie. I walked into meet a client for the first time. The client told me to take my tie off! They said that the only people who wore ties in their office were the tax collector and the auditors, and they did not like either one of them. So, if I wanted to be liked, the tie needed to come off. So, the tie came off. Now when I visit my clients, I am always wearing a suit, but I do not wear a tie. I only had the one client say something to me, but I was able to look at my clients when I met them and gauge how they dressed. Most of my clients are in slacks and button-down shirts. I have a few that may have a tie on. But none wear a suit every day. The key to dressing this way is to make sure your customer is comfortable. If someone comes into a place of business and is overdressed or underdressed, it could make the prospect or the client uncomfortable. For example, when I worked for Black and Decker, most of my sales calls happened on a job site. If I were to walk onto a job site in a suit and tie, not only would I be a safety issue, I would have made my clients and prospects extremely nervous.

But when I say that every day is an interview, I am referring to the third dress code you need to pay attention to. This is the off-duty dress code. Quite honestly, I don't think you are ever really off-duty. I travel a lot for my job and spend many mornings and late evenings on airplanes. Many of my co-workers and many other sales professionals that I know will run to the closest bathroom as soon as their last meeting is over and change into comfortable clothes. They switch into shorts or sweatpants, based on the weather, and get comfortable. While I can understand getting comfortable and most times the people do not look unpresentable- I challenge you to always view yourself as if you are at an interview. You never know who you may be sitting beside on a plane, train, or Uber. I was sitting next to a Regional Sales Manager for a medical device company a few years back. We started talking about our jobs, travelling, and how we missed our family. After a while, he asked me what I did for a living and I told him. We started talking sales and the next thing I knew, he was offering me his card and saying we should set up a job interview! We were both dressed in suits. It is entirely possible that the conversation could have happened if I were dressed in more comfortable clothes, but that is a risk I do not recommend you take.

Also, when you are out on the weekends or after work, you never know who you may see. Not only does your dress need to appear professional but so does your behavior. Imagine if you are a financial advisor in a small town and go out to the local bar and act like a fool. One of the biggest targets you were trying to land had agreed to meet with you the next week, but after seeing your behavior at the bar, he decided to cancel your meeting because he does not want you managing his money. Take my word for it: something like this can happen, and it will hurt your business.

Treat every day as if it were an interview and be prepared to meet people no matter where you are. You never know what may happen, whom you will meet, or where you might meet them.

When my wife and I first got married I worked for Black and Decker. They provided us with a company truck. The only downside to this truck was it had the company logo plastered all over it. On most Friday nights we would go out to dinner, I would still be in my company shirt which also had the Black and Decker logo on it. It never failed that someone would come up to me and ask if I worked for Black and Decker. The smart-ass in me wanted to answer...nope just a big fan. But I always said that I did, and this person would start talking about our tools and how much he loved our tools. Initially my wife was irritated by the intrusion, but I had to remind her that these people are ultimately paying for this dinner through their purchases and a bad experience with me could impact the business. You must always be on.

In addition to how you dress for work and even for non-work events, you need to think about how you look in this digital world. From a professional perspective, your LinkedIn profile is the place to put your best foot forward. According to Professor Dawn Edmiston of The College of William and Mary's Mason School of Business, the following steps can be performed to provide you with a better online presence.[3]

> **(1) Have a personalized LinkedIn URL.** My LinkedIn profile is: www.linkedin.com/in/bohamrick. Dr. Edmiston's profile is www.linkedin.com/in/dawnedmiston. You can find more information on how to this by following the steps here: https://help.linkedin.com/app/answers/detail/a_id/87. Having a personalized URL helps with your brand image and makes you easier to locate in search engines.

---

[3] Compiled from a video interview with Dr. Dawn Edmiston seen here https://youtu.be/6EyXdmc9Ly8

(2) **Feature a professional profile photo.** You have two options here. (1) Hire someone to take your headshot. This will cost a couple hundred dollars at the most but will be well worth the investment. (2) Find a friend that is an aspiring photographer or photojournalist and have them take the photo for you. You can see my photo on my LinkedIn page. You will notice that I use the same picture for LinkedIn and Twitter as well as on my website. Having a consistent image makes it easier for people to find you. You also have the option of a background photo on LinkedIn. I use a photo provided by my employer, but you could use something that speaks to your interest from a professional perspective.

(3) **Create a headline that reflects the value you provide to others.** My headline reads: "Bo Hamrick is an Enterprise Account Manager in the Southeast US. Providing clients, the freedom from the single stack." I would like for yours to be simple, include your name (helps with Search Engine Optimization) but provide a little bit of intrigue.

(4) **Develop a summary that clearly articulates your brand promise.** In other words, who are you? Mine is: "My name is Bo Hamrick, and I am a seasoned veteran in the field of sales, business development and account management. Helping real estate companies of all sizes and in the Southeastern United States to dramatically grow their business

and increase profitability. My management skills and leadership continue to deliver results for organizations looking to expand their reach and revenues. In my current role, I am responsible for all enterprise level clients in the Commercial Real Estate Market in the Southeastern United States and the Caribbean at MRI Software. I drive revenue growth, manage the account relationship, manage current projects and collaborate with our clients to develop innovative, value creating solutions. With 15 years of experience driving sales growth, I am an experienced business leader who inspires organizational adoption of strategies, drives revenue, manages operational execution, achieves critical business objectives and creates a sustainable winning relationship with my clients. I am a highly motivated and goal-oriented sales professional who constantly seeks to further his knowledge and experience. I have been described as confidently assertive, self-motivated, compassionate, and efficient. I have a strong appetite for learning and looking for any opportunity available to enhance my knowledge and situational awareness. In May of 2018, I will graduate from The College of William And Mary's Mason School of Business with an MBA. I am on LinkedIn to strengthen business relations, ensure customer success and help lead the sales team of my company. In addition, I like to mentor younger reps and take pride in seeing them reach their full potential as a sales professional, and more importantly as a human being. Feel free to reach out if I can ever be of any assistance to your or your organization. I may not be able to help everyone, but I will work tirelessly to find someone who can help you." This summary has no limit on the number of characters and you are free to be as short or as long as you feel necessary.

(5) Once you have done these few basic steps, you need to track your performance on social media. In the last chapter of the book I will provide some insight on some social media tools you should use.[4] You want to look at how many followers you have, and which way are they trending. You would also want to see how many views your posts are getting. You want to post valuable information for your prospects and clients on your social media channels and it is important to understand when and what types of posts generate more traffic.

4   Edmiston, Dawn. Thanks to LinkedIn my Dream Job Found Me. (https://www.linkedin.com/pulse/thanks-linkedin-my-dream-job-found-me-when-i-looking-dawn-edmiston/)

HAVE A MENTOR

We herd sheep, we drive cattle, and we lead people. Lead me, follow me, or get out of my way.
—*George S. Patton*

LOOKING FOR A BOOST IN your career? Find yourself a mentor. A mentor is that one person who can guide you, help you, take you under his wing, and nurture your career. A Yoda to your Luke Skywalker. A Glinda the Good Witch to your Dorothy Gale. What separates a mentor from the average professional contact is a long-term commitment and deep-seated investment in your future.

I would like to add what a mentor is not. A mentor is not your manager; he/she is not here to tell you what to do all the time or to train you. So, what is a mentor used for?

Where a typical professional contact might be associated with quick introductions, exchanges of business cards, and phone calls, and your relationship with a mentor likely involves long lunches and time spent in the office of the mentor. A mentor can be someone that you vent to. Do not forget, though, that your mentor is more experienced than you and has a day job they need to perform, so you need to keep the venting to a minimum. But your mentor is a good person to talk with about strategy and helping to prepare for sales meetings. All these things will help accelerate your sales abilities. A mentor is often in a position you'd like to be in and has the clout and connections to guide you to a similar position. As you look at each chapter in the book, your mentor can be a resource for you. Do you need someone to help you with your sales presentation? Could you benefit from doing a role play? Do you have questions about how to dress for a presentation? Do you think you are stuck on the sales roller coaster? All of these are great opportunities for your mentor to be of assistance.

Hopefully you see the benefit of a mentor. Now the question I typically hear from new hires is, "How do I get a mentor?" The answer to that is simple enough; you just need to ask! Whom you ask is the more important question. You should consider all the following possibilities: your current company, your alma mater, your circle of friends and family and your professional organizations.

In your current company, look for someone who has followed a career path you would like to emulate. This could be someone who is just a few years older than you and who is not too far removed from your current role and who can help you navigate your company's corporate ladder and political landscape. Another option is if you can develop a great relationship with one of the senior executives, and if you have shown promise within the organization, you should ask one of them. However, if you are going the senior executive route, you need to keep two things in mind. First, make sure your boss is aware and gives you the go ahead to ask the senior executive, and second, be prepared to really work hard with this type of mentor. You will be thrusted into the forefront of this person's mind and need to always be putting your best foot forward.

Asking a person a few years older than you is the less risky of the two options and will most likely provide you with the most actionable assistance. When I mentor new reps at my company, I am in the trenches with them and understand the questions and concerns they typically face with our clients. Senior executives are many times too far removed from the clients to be able to help you. The downfall to having a junior associate mentor is they have little say, typically, in promotions and showcasing your abilities to them will have little impact on your career advancement.

The senior leader in your organization will not provide you with as much tactical assistance as a junior leader, but they provide value for you by giving you a high-level view of strategic approaches and if you can demonstrate your capabilities to the senior leader, you have a better chance of speeding up your career advancement.

When looking for a mentor from your school, there are a few options. Did you belong to a social or academic fraternity or sorority? Were you a member of an organization like Fellowship of Christian Athletes, Student Government, or a sports team? Was there a sales club at your school? If you can answer yes to any of these, you have a network you could tap into. Was there a person who was a year or two older than you who has a job that you would like to attain or has followed a similar career path as you would like to do? There are many different avenues you could explore to find the right person for you.

Do your parents have friends, or do you have family members who have been in sales? Is there someone who was like a parental figure for you when growing up that you can call on? Having someone who has been in sales a long time like this can pay huge dividends when you are just getting started in your sales career. I remember during my first job, I had a family friend who was flying into Boston, MA for a business meeting and he had some spare time, so we scheduled time to catch up and grab a drink. He was not my mentor in any official sense, but for a couple of hours, I was able to pick his brain and learn more from him about being a lifelong sales professional than any book was ever able to teach me. Of course, my book had not been written yet.

Are you a member of a professional or civic organization? This could be your church, Rotary, Chamber of Commerce, or even an adult sports league. Basically, anyone with whom you come in contact in a professional or semi-professional way falls into this category. Make sure that this person can provide you with all the key deliverables mentioned above.

The final thing to consider when selecting a mentor is to be able to provide the mentor with a compelling reason why they should take time out their busy day to talk with you. When the mentor is internal to your organization, the reason is easy to explain. If your mentor can get some form of credit for helping you succeed, that should be compelling enough of a reason for them to help you out. That credit could be compensation based on your sales; it could be a bonus for being a mentor, or at the very least, a feather in their cap for when they are looking to get a promotion. Any of these could be the compelling reason for them to want to help you. For those outside of your organization, the feather in the hat approach may not be good enough, but hopefully as you talk with them, you can find what drives them and they will remember that they were also once new in this field and will want to help you.

Is there anything else you should look for in a mentor? You should work with someone that you can respect, and your mentor should respect you as well. You should have a good feel after a few meetings as to whether the rapport is right for a valuable relationship. The group, Women Unlimited, suggests that mentored relationships benefit when the mentee approaches the mentoring with openness, honesty, introspection, realistic expectations, accountability, and the ability to admit mistakes and share failures.[5] Jeffrey Patnaude, author of *Leading from the Maze*, also suggest that mentors possess emotional intelligence, intuition, a drive to keep learning and a desire to bring about change.[6]

Typically, if your Human Resources department or sales management team is involved in your mentorship program, you would have a formal mentor program. For example, at

---

[5] https://www.livecareer.com/career/advice/jobs/mentor-value
[6] Patnaude, Jeff. *Leading from the Maze*. Ten Speed Press

my current employer, there is a formal mentor program. Top sales talent who have been flagged for potential advancement are asked to be mentors to newer sales professionals. As I mentioned above, the mentor has a reason for wanting to be a part of this program, so they can prove their worth as a sales manager. But these types of programs are not offered at every company. Most companies that I have worked for had an informal mentor program. In these situations, either the mentee or the mentor initiated the relationship, and for some reason or another, they hit it off together and both were able to help the other.

Regardless of how much you take away from this book, this chapter may be one of the most important. You are new to sales; you are not expected to know everything. While this book may provide you with a few pointers, each company is different, and every sales environment is different. You can greatly increase your performance as a sales professional if you have a mentor.

The key to nurturing this relationship is communication. Talk with your mentor about mutual expectations for the relationship and how it will work, what it will look like, and how often you will communicate. Be sure not to overburden your mentor by demanding too much time and attention or becoming overly dependent. When I work with my mentees, we have a weekly meeting for 30 minutes to discuss things the mentee wants to discuss. In addition, I am available via phone, text and email to address anything that arises during the week.

The mentor may tend to give you a lot more than you do to the relationship, so find ways that you can regularly express your gratitude and let the mentor know you value their time and appreciate their guidance. I must admit the feeling of being needed and sense of making a difference in mentees life is typically rewarding enough for me to want to do more for the mentee. If you feel obliged, you can send a token of your appreciation, I had a mentor send me a book for my kids. I thought that was great because I knew the mentee was listening to me and how important my kids are to me. You can also send a note to your mentor's manager, letting them know how thankful you are for your mentor's contribution to your professional growth.

There are two additional types of mentors we should discuss. I have not personally used either of these, and quite frankly, I am torn on the matter. The first would be a paid mentor. You pay someone for mentoring or coaching assistance. I would not really call this a mentorship but rather a business relationship. Instead of it being a mentor, this is just a sales coach. There is nothing wrong with having a sales coach, but you need to make sure whatever you are paying for this either is reimbursed by your company or will make you enough money in commissions to offset the expense.

The second would be a mastermind group. A mastermind group is when a group of like-minded individuals meet on a consistent basis to discuss topics and help each other with problems. In some mastermind groups, the facilitator is paid by the other members for being in charge and because of the pay factor, I categorize this as a business relationship as well.

Both types of relationships could be beneficial, and I am not going to say to avoid this route, but please make sure you are getting your money's worth. Again, you need to look at this as a return on investment. If you spend $100.00 a month for a mastermind or a sales coach, how much of an increase in commissions do you need to see to justify the expense? Do you need to double your money? Would a 10X increase in your investment justify your time and money? If you can determine the return on your investment that you need to see, you will be able to measure how successful this has been for you.

JUST BECAUSE YOUR PRODUCT IS GREAT, DOES NOT MEAN YOU WILL MAKE THE SALE.

It is not necessary to do extraordinary things to get extraordinary results.
—Warren Buffett

SALES AUTHOR JEFFREY GITOMER SAYS, "All things being equal, people buy from people they like. All things not being quite so equal, people buy from people they like." What Gitomer is alluding to is that even if your product is not the cheapest or best, you can still make the sale because people are going to buy from the individuals they like. Think about the last time you bought a car. There are Chevrolet, Ford, Honda, and Toyota dealerships in every city in America. There is a high likelihood that you could drive less than 30 minutes and find at least two dealers selling the same car. Why do people choose one over the other? They are literally selling the exact same product. So why? People find a car salesperson they like! If you have a good experience with that salesperson and need to buy another car, you are most likely going to go to that same person again. Let me give you another example...Cell Phone Service. I can buy an iPhone from Verizon, Sprint, T-Mobile, AT&T, or some other cellular provider and can have an iPhone work on their network. The phone I receive is the same phone. Depending on which provider you talk to, the networks may not be quite so equal, but you choose the provider you like, even if it is more expensive or less reliable than the other ones.

Think about yourself. Why did you pick the car dealership you picked? Why did you pick the cell phone service you picked? How about the grocery store you shop in? In most cases, people choose these things based on what they like.

Here is a real-life example that happened to me the other day. I have been banking with the same bank for my checking and savings account since at least 2004. I have a checking account, a savings account for our family and a savings account for each of my kids. I like my bank. Their app is easy to use, I can deposit checks from my phone. For the one time each year that I need to walk into the branch it is close enough to be convenient. I get a cold call from one of the personal bankers at the branch. When I say hello, she responds in an overly happy tone (picture a cheerleader who has just inhaled helium from a balloon and drank 3 Red Bulls.) She says, "Why hello Mr. Hamrick this is Rita from

<Insert Bank Name>. How are you today?" By this point in the conversation, I am already regretting answering this call. After exchanging some pleasantries, Rita goes into her sales pitch.

RITA: "Mr. Hamrick, the reason for **MY** call today is because **I** think **I** can help you have more money." (Note everywhere in this conversation that I have a word in all caps and bolded, Rita really emphasized that word.)

ME: "Really, you are going to just give me more money?"

RITA: "**I** am prohibited from telling you over the phone **ALL of** the wonderful things **I** can do, so I would like for you to come see **ME** at the branch in town."

At this point I was turned off completely. Her words were all about her and what she could do. Think back to chapter one, she thought this call was all about her. Then comes the line that she is prohibited from telling me over the phone...WHAT? She called me...ON THE PHONE! Rita's script was all about her and draped in a shroud of mystery. It was a tactic to get me in the door of the branch. But it did little to motivate me to want to come into the branch. Look, I am no dummy. I know they can see my transaction history and they see that every month I make a mortgage payment to one of their competitors. The bank can also see that I just got my tax return from Uncle SAM and it was sitting in my savings account. They either wanted me to refinance my mortgage or put some of my savings account money into a different account.

So, I threw an objection her way. I told her that I work Monday through Friday and could not take off to come to the branch. Rita had a few options: (1) Agree to meet on a Saturday at the Branch, (2) Offer to come to my house and meet, (3) schedule a time to talk on the phone, or (4) Push back and stick to her Monday through Friday timeslot.

RITA: "**I** must meet you in **MY** office, it is **OUR** policy."

ME: "Well Rita, I guess I can't meet with you then."

RITA: "Ok, Mr. Hamrick, I will send you an email with a link that will allow you to schedule a meeting with me at your convenience."

What? I can't meet with you does not mean that you should send me an email with a link to schedule a meeting. Let's just say that email was deleted and never responded to. The sad thing for Rita was that I was driving from Charlotte, NC to Virginia and had about four more hours of driving to go. If she had asked me if now was a good time to talk, I would have told her yes. I was a captive audience for the next 4 hours. If she had given me an example of what she was alluding to instead of keeping it a mystery, I would have given her a chance to pitch.

Aside from the failure to talk about what is in it for me and not handling the objection well, the biggest thing that Rita did wrong was she hid behind a policy. If you find yourself saying, "It's our policy," what the customer is hearing is: "Our policy is to piss you off and we do not care about you." Your policy should be to wow customers and leave them feeling happy.

I know what you are thinking: "Bo, I work in B2B sales or B2G sales. They are different than someone picking out their cell phone or choosing a grocery store or a banker calling you at home." You can think that if you want, but I would tell you, you are wrong. Even if the purchase goes through a request for proposal (RFP), someone is writing that RFP, and if you can be the person who helps with that RFP, then you have a better chance of being selected. If you can be more liked than your competitors, then you have the chance of being the person asked to help with the RFP. In his book, *The New Solution Selling*, Keith Eades talks about being column fodder.[7] Basically what Eades is talking about is if a company is doing an evaluation to buy a product, they typically have a first choice, but since the company requires them to look at multiple products, they add a few more companies as column fodder to make it look like they evaluated multiple options. If you are column fodder, you do not have a good chance of winning. If you want to be in the first column, you need to be the one they like, personally.

What can you do to be more likeable? First, remember that no one cares about you. Your interactions with your prospects and clients need to be focused on them. You need to provide a value to them. Are your face – to – face interactions enjoyable and providing value? Then they will like you. Are your emails and phone calls appropriate, or are you wasting their time? Do you allow them to talk about their family? Do you have sincerity and authenticity? All of these are things that will make you more likable. The single most important action you can do to be more likeable is to listen to your prospects and customers!

---

[7] The New Solution Selling. Eades, Keith. 2004. McGraw-Hill

Ron Willingham in his book *Authenticity, The Head, Heart and Soul of Selling* says, "Successful selling is doing things for people, not to them. Helping instead of persuading. Serving instead of being served."[8] I would recommend this book. In it he discusses 6 steps to the sales cycle.

1. Connect: Build comfort, trust and rapport with clients.
2. Listen: Determine their needs, wants or desired solutions.
3. Illustrate: Demonstrate your ability to meet their needs.
4. Evaluate: Come to agreement with the client that your solutions are right.
5. Negotiate: Uncover objections and find solutions to them.
6. Transact: Exchange your solution for payment.

---

[8] Authenticity, The Head, Heart and Soul of Selling. Willingham, Ron. 2014 Prentice Hall Press

THE TOP IS A LONELY PLACE

Winning isn't everything but wanting to win is.
—Vince Lombardi

WHEN I WAS GROWING UP and playing sports in the backyard, I always had the same scenario running through my head. I am batting for the Atlanta Braves; it is Game Seven of the World Series, bottom of the ninth. We are down by three runs; the bases are loaded, two outs, full count, three balls and two strikes. It comes down to this last pitch. If I hit a Grand Slam Home Run, we win the World Series. The crowd is standing and cheering. The whole stadium is yelling my name. Here's the pitch. I swing; CRACK; bat hits ball; the ball is flying to deep left field, and it is going, going, GONE! Grand Slam Home Run! The Braves win! The Braves Win! THE BRAVES WIN! I round third base and head for home, the crowd is going wild, and all my teammates are there to give me a high five! If your childhood was anything like mine, you had some similar dream. The sports team or the sport may have been different. But we all dreamed of being the hero and having our teammates there to celebrate with us.

In a lot of ways, sales and sports are similar. But there is one big difference. If you close a big deal that allows you to reach your quarter or year-end goal, or even better, close a big deal that allows the organization to reach its sales goals, you will most likely not be met with your team of sales professionals standing around the office, ready to pop champagne with you! If you would like a sense of what it would be like, Google "teammates not celebrating a home run." You will find countless videos of a batter tagging home plate and heading to the dugout only to find his teammates ignoring him completely. In most cases the teammates are trying to be funny. However, Sales can be a selfish sport. As you are bringing in the big deals and big bucks, your teammates are bringing in the excuses. They are going to say:

"You had the better territory."

"You had the better leads."

"Our manager likes you better."

"You got lucky!"

The excuses are intended to bring you down. They will come in hot and heavy. Be ready for it. Don't let them get to you.

The worst experience that I ever had was when I really felt like I had hit a grand slam for my company and for my yearly quota. I had a client that used us for a portion of their business, but there was still opportunity for us to pick up more of their business. One of two things was going to happen at the end of this particular sales opportunity. The client was going to either expand their use of our products, and I would hit the proverbial home run, or they were going to leave us and use one of our competitors. That would have been equal to me striking out in the bottom of the ninth. I went through a tough three-month sales process with multiple demonstrations and phone calls, both internally and with the client. We had a long, drawn out negotiation over pricing, and ultimately, won the business. I was the first to recognize that this deal was a team win. It took many people from many different divisions in our company to help me close this deal. But within days of the deal closing, I heard from people in the sales organization that they too would hit their number if their clients handed them big orders. I also heard that I got lucky and did not deserve the credit I was receiving. I was devastated. This deal was won because of a lot of hard work from many people in our organization...not just me! Nothing was handed to our company; nothing was just handed to me. We worked our butts off. As much as those other people's comments upset me about my efforts. I was really irritated for all those other people who also worked hard to win this business. The detractors were not giving them any credit either.

IF YOU ARE FEMALE, I have more bad news for you. You are going to get it worse than men do. I am sorry; it is truly not my fault that this the case, but you need to be ready for it. As you read this chapter, I want you to think about the men on your sales team. Close your eyes and think of each one of them. Now I want you to realize that the excuses are not going to come from them. They are going to come from the other women in your organization. Women are tougher on each other than men are on other men.

Here is a real-life story. The names have been changed to protect the innocent. I was recently talking to an ex-colleague of mine and we were updating each other on how our year was going. This ex-colleague, call her Laura, asked me if anyone had been promoted recently. I told her that Cindy had been promoted. I let her know what the position was, who else interviewed for it, and how Cindy was doing in her new role. The first words out of Laura's mouth were, "I guess it helps when you sleep with some of the big wigs!" There were no congratulations for Cindy, no good for her, nothing. Laura went straight for the jugular and accused Cindy of sleeping her way to the top. The crazy thing is, Cindy had won three straight president club trips, had mentored other successful sales reps, and had really put together a great game plan for the position, if she were hired. None of that mattered to Laura because she had excuses for all of Cindy's successes along the way.

I'm not telling you this story to make sure you do not talk negatively about other reps, but rather to prepare you for when you have your bottom of the ninth, two outs, Grand Slam moment and do not have your teammates there to celebrate with you. Instead of being upset with your lack of support from your teammates, you have the power to celebrate your successes with your family, friends, manager, and mentor.

DON'T BE A JACK OF ALL TRADES AND A MASTER OF NONE

What we dwell on is who we become.
—Oprah Winfrey

E ARLIER WE TALKED ABOUT THE sales roller coaster and how important tracking your sales activity can be. Earlier, I also shared with you a sample activity list.

Dials	Meetings	Demo	Negotiate	Sales	Avg $ / Sale
200	20	10	5	2	$100.00

I want you to now look at these numbers as an average across all reps in your company. In this activity tracker, the company average says if you make 200 dials that will ultimately lead to two sales. What you will find as you start your career is that you will not follow the exact numbers listed above. You may make 200 dials, get 15 meetings, seven demos, six negotiations and two sales. Does it really matter if that happens? No – But the key is to look at where you are strong and where you are weak. In my example, I am below average in converting dials into meetings, roughly average in getting meetings into demos, above average in getting demos to move to negotiate, and below average in getting negotiations into sales. Many sales managers will want to work on the two areas where you are below average and try to make you average. Or a jack of all trades. I would challenge you to focus on the areas where you are above average and make those areas of the sales cycle even better. If I can move from seven demos going to six negotiations and make it seven for seven, then every two months I make an additional sale...based on the averages. As your sales manager, I would focus on making you a master of at least one of the steps in the sales process and then start bringing up your abilities in another to average or above average task. In addition, if you can increase your dials to 300 or 400 in the example, you have a good chance of increasing your sales from two per week to three or four.

There is a psychological benefit to working on improving things that you are good at. Let's look at sports again. If you have never set foot on a golf course before, you may make major improvements with just a few short lessons, but you will still be pretty bad. For a person who has played golf for several years who takes a number of lessons and focuses on a key area, not only will their game improve, but the golfer will be more satisfied with his/her improvements and will stick with the training regimen. A non-golfer, on the other hand, will still get frustrated with his lack of overall improvement.

Once you are proficient on one of the steps in the sales process, then we start working on the next stage that has the highest success rate. Let me give you another sports example from the world of golf. Let's say that you are a decent golfer and go to a pro for some training. The training could go one of two ways. In the first example, you take a few swings on the driving range. The pro then rattles off, "Spread your legs further, square your shoulders up, keep you left arm straight, keep your head down, etc." This would be the shotgun approach to fixing your game. You may remember to do one or two things that the pro tells you, but it is highly unlikely for you to remember all the tips the pro has given you. The second scenario would be that you hit a few shots for the pro. The pro then gives you one task: "Tilt your hips back." Then the pro would have you hit 100 balls focusing on that one tip. After this tweak or enhancement has become common for you because of muscle memory, then the pro would provide you with the next tip.

I want you to take the same approach as the second golf pro with your sales training and sales ability. By mastering your skills, you will be a more consistently producing sales professional. This is a slower path to improvement but will also provide you with sustainable growth over the long haul.

So, first find your strengths and weaknesses. Then find the tasks you enjoy doing and starting with your strongest, most enjoyable task, select one tip or trick that you can focus on to improve your sales ability.

Another advantage of this approach is that there are decades of scientific research that shows one of the key drivers to your motivation level is your ability to master the skills required to be successful in your job. Seeking mastery has a far greater impact on your job satisfaction than your pay does.

UNCOMFORTABLE IS NORMAL

You miss 100% of the shots you don't take.
—Wayne Gretzky

I WAS CALLING ON A local franchise of a fast food restaurant group in my area. I knew the owner's name was Nick. (The name again has been changed to protect the innocent.) I called the store and asked for Nick. Surprisingly, he answered the phone. I introduced myself, "Hi Nick, this is Bo from..." Before I could complete the sentence, he says, "Not Interested!" He abruptly hung up the phone on me. I immediately called him back and when he answered I said, "I am sorry Nick. I think we got disconnected. My name is Bo Hamrick and I work with..." Again, before I could finish the sentence, he said he was not interested and hung up on me. After the second call, since I was close to his office, I decided to stop by and try a face – to – face call. I was led back to Nick's office, and this time when I started, I said, "Nick, I would like to buy your business!"

Before I tell you what his response was...why did I ask him that? I figured this guy had hung up on me twice. He says he is not interested. If I keep doing what I had been doing, I was not going to make the sale. I had nothing to lose. I went in there knowing I was not going to make the sale if I started with a typical sales pitch. If I asked to buy his business, one of three things were going to happen. He was going to throw me out of his office and I would not make the sale; he was going to sell me his business and I would not need to make the sale, or he was going to stop and listen and maybe I would make the sale. Well, he stopped what he was doing and looked at me and said, "What did you say?" I introduced myself and told him that I had called him twice because we were doing an employee gift purchase and wanted to purchase gift cards from him totaling $10,000 and that my company had been able to save other companies like his upwards of $10,000 per year. So, if he was not interested in making $10,000 and not interested in saving $10,000, then that seemed like the kind of business I wanted to buy. I will admit, the closing line was a bit cheesy, but I had nothing to lose. He had already hung up on me twice, so I decided to go for it. The story ended happily ever after. They signed with us a week later, and now I have a great story to tell for life. The best part was after we signed the contract, he asked about the $10,000 we were going to spend on gift cards. As quickly as I could I thought of one of his competitors and said, "Sorry Nick, as soon as you told me the second time you were not interested, we called <Competitor> and bought the gift cards from them." I said it with a sly little smile on my face and he just grinned at me knowing that we were not buying any gift cards.

The take away from the story is not to go around trying to buy your prospect's businesses but to get comfortable being uncomfortable. Also, we were not looking to buy $10,000 worth of gift cards either! I do not condone lying to prospects or customers, but I wanted to make the prospect a little uncomfortable as well (after all, I was uncomfortable being hung up on) and it happened to work in this scenario.

Sales is uncomfortable. You are calling people and interrupting their day. You are basically asking them out on a blind date. If you can get them to meet with you, then both parties go through a dance of asking and answering questions. You are forced to attempt to develop a relationship with a stranger. Then you go into the negotiation where any good negotiator tells you that if you speak first, you lose. So many times, two people end up staring at each other...that is uncomfortable.

The best way to become comfortable doing uncomfortable things is to practice. I do not mean that you do one training or one role play with your boss but that you need to practice these common objections and scenarios in your business on a weekly basis.

I was ready to make the second call to Nick and use the, "I'm sorry I think we got disconnected," line because I had practiced that line in role plays during my training for what seemed like a hundred times. You need to practice handling objections and overcoming roadblocks in the sales process. When you do the role play, I would challenge you to have your boss or a peer of yours do it with you and have them be as difficult as possible to close. The harder they are, the harder you will have to work to overcome them and the more uncomfortable you will feel. But as you become better at overcoming the difficult questions, you will be able to handle the easier objections.

I still remember one trainer I had during my career at Black and Decker. His name was Dick Redpath. Dick if you are out there, thank you for all that you did for everyone who ever came through Black and Decker University. Dick was from Scotland and had a thick Scottish accent. But more importantly, he was hard. When I went through training, so many of my colleagues were scared to death to face Dick Redpath in a roleplay. He would come up with objections that he had not talked about or that were not part of the classroom training portion. He challenged me to always think on my feet and be ready for whatever the customer or prospect threw at me. So again, Dick, you are the man and thank you from the bottom of my heart.

Aside from practicing these scenarios, another way of being successful is to have a process to handle objections. One that I learned very early on in my career was called the AIA method. AIA stood for Acknowledge, Identify, and Answer. For example: "(Acknowledge) I can understand how you feel that way, (Identify) In fact I had a recent customer feel the same way as you, (Answer) and they found (Inset value statement)." By practicing the AIA method repeatedly, it will reduce the uncomfortable feeling the sentence may have the first time you try it and the uncomfortable feeling you get because you received the objection. It will also make it easier for you to respond to your prospects or customer.

You need to find the parts of the sales process that make you most uncomfortable and then work with your manager, mentor or peers to help overcome those uncomfortable feelings and improve upon them.

HOMEWORK ALERT I want you to go out and be a buyer tonight. I want you to return the favor and make a sales professional feel uncomfortable. The next time you buy anything from a cup of coffee to a new car or house, I want you to make it uncomfortable for the person selling to you. Ask for a 10% discount. Now don't cheat with this one. If you are military or have a student ID, do not use them! I want you to ask for a discount for no good reason and see if they will do it. Of course, part of the exercise is to find a good reason for the discount. Just don't use a discount card or because of your class (Military, Student, Senior Citizen, etc.) Find a valid reason you should receive the discount. If you get denied, I want you to keep practicing until you get the discount. Then share your story on Twitter and tweet me @bohamrick and use #10%discount so we can all keep track. Also share how much your 10% discount saved you. So that companies do not catch on to our homework assignment, let's keep the name of the business out of the tweet!

If you are going to be successful in this homework assignment, you need to be prepared and ready for the objections. Why are you asking for a discount? Why are you deserving of a discount? What things are they going to say when you ask for a discount? Of course, I would be remiss if I didn't tell you to roleplay this with someone before you try it in an actual business.

I was at my company's annual conference one year and was at the coffee shop. I was buying eight cups of coffee to share with some co-workers. I asked the cashier if I could have a 25% discount since I was buying eight cups. She looked at me like I was crazy, but I told her I was serious, so she asked her manager and they gave it to me. I would have never received the discount if I had not asked for it...no matter how uncomfortable it felt. This request of a volume discount is typically the easiest.

Another time when I was given this homework assignment, I was out of town on business and was given the exact same instructions. I was told to negotiate something in the local mall that night. I went to one of the kiosks in the middle of the mall. You know the ones where they attack you with some lotion or jewelry cleaner and squirt your hand with their product. I always hated how aggressive they were, so I figured if I could get a discount from them, I would be happy to at least make their commission a bit smaller. I went through his sales pitch and listened. This sales professional did a poor job of qualifying me. I had no need or want that his lotion was going to solve for. He created no personal connection and was obnoxious. After he went through his pitch and gave me his price, I looked at him and said he was crazy...That was too expensive. The game was on! He talked, we haggled, he offered more product, and I pretended to walk away. Finally, at the very end of our sales call together, he offered a 50% discount on a travel kit, and I bought it.

By putting yourself in the shoes of the buyer, this gives you a glimpse into the positions you place your prospects and clients in. Aside from practicing the art of being uncomfortable, you gain access into the minds of your prospects and clients and can start to understand how they feel. This too will make you more prepared when you go into your next negotiation with a client or prospect.

PREPARATION IS PARAMOUNT

*Give me six hours to chop down a tree and
I will spend the first four sharpening the
axe.*
—Abraham Lincoln

THERE IS A COMMON SAYING for those who run that says: "The most difficult step of any run is the first one out the door." The premise of this statement is if you can just get out the door and go on a run, it will get easier. Many running coaches will recommend their clients create a ritual of getting your running clothes laid out the day before and setting yourself up inside the house for success so that once you take that first step out the door, you will go on a run.

For sales, there is a similar thought process. In order to be successful in sales, you need to set yourself up for success. Setting yourself up for success in running means laying your workout clothes out the night before. In sales, it means that you are prepared for every meeting, presentation, and call block that you have on your schedule. Preparation is paramount to your success in sales. When you are first getting started, you will believe in preparation, but as you gain more experience, you will find yourself skipping the planning phases because this presentation is just like all the others you have given in the past. Please avoid this trap.

What are some steps you can do to get prepared? Let's take a look at the activity tracker I have referenced in the book already.

Dials	Meetings	Demo	Negotiate	Sales	Avg $ / Sale
200	20	10	5	2	$100.00

Each stage of the sales process should have certain steps you need to complete to move to the next stage, and in each stage, you need to be prepared to complete each step while this example is generic, you should be able to gather enough examples to apply this to your sales process

The Dials Step

In the dials step, you are either making phone calls, sending emails, knocking on doors, or some combination of the above. For the sake of brevity and simplicity, let's assume you are only making phone calls, and you are going to sit down for a couple of hours on Monday to make these calls. In preparation for this time on my calendar, I would do the following steps:

1. Identify the 200 individuals I want to call

2. Create a spreadsheet of their names, company, title, and phone number. Your company may also offer a Customer Relationship Management (CRM) software to help you with this.

3. If possible, I would then rank them based on size or potential dollars in sales and start with the highest ones first.

4. Depending on your phone script: either you are going to reference similar companies that you have been able to help, or you will reference key benefits your company can deliver to the target. I would have those written out in the spreadsheet. So that for example, if I am calling on a restaurant and want to reference other restaurants in the area, I would have them listed so I could rattle them off very quickly.

By following these steps in preparation, I should be able to call one right after another with an attempt to schedule them for a meeting. Additional things I would do to get prepared are make sure my workspace is clean, my email is turned off, and social media and other distractions are eliminated. I would then have my calendar laid out with my spreadsheet of targets and have my scripts in front of me.

By following these simple steps, you will be ready to be successful in the dial stage of the sales process.

The Meeting Step

Once you have the meetings arranged, you will need to be prepared for executing on the meeting. Now every company and every sales process could be different here. You could be presenting to a large group or to a single person. You need to know who you are presenting to and in what format. For the restaurant example I mentioned earlier, most likely I would be sitting at a table in the restaurant, talking to the target. Currently, I call on real estate companies. Almost all my meetings occur in a conference room. Some of the preparation steps you need to take are:

1. Research who will be in attendance. Do they have a LinkedIn profile, twitter handle or Facebook page? What is their role in the organization? To whom do they report? Have you looked at the company website to see their structure?

2. Research the company. What are their strategic goals? Do they have a mission statement? Have they been in the news recently for either good or bad things? One way to get this information is to set up Google Alerts for all your prospects and clients.

3. What do you want to present? How are you going to present it? Do you need handouts, leave-behinds, or are you bring some swag with you?

4. What are you trying to sell during this meeting? Many sales reps botch this part up. In an initial meeting, you are not actually trying to sell your product. You are trying to get them interested enough to buy with their time, another meeting. In my example, that is when you would demonstrate your abilities. When I worked at Cintas, it was possible that it could happen on the same call. Now that I work in an enterprise software environment, a one call close is not possible to do. Make sure you know what is normal for your business.

Each of the following steps in my example: Demo, Negotiate, Close, and Sell will really depend on what is going on with the account in the first couple of steps. You never want to wing a presentation, phone call or any interaction with your prospect or clients. You need to be prepared. Similar questions you need to ask yourself in each of the following steps are: Who should be involved? What role will each person play? What do we want to accomplish during the meeting? What will the next steps be? What do I plan on saying, and what are all the possible responses my client or prospect could give me? How would I respond to all the prospect's comments?

I would like to share a personal story where I thought I was prepared but had missed a key step. I was dating the young woman who ultimately became my wife. We had been dating almost two years, and I was ready to propose to her. Now, I am a bit old fashioned and so is my wife's family. So, I knew I would have to ask my wife's dad for his permission to marry his daughter. I also wanted to ask him! So, I started preparing for every step of this "sales process." I picked the weekend that Leslie and I would travel to her parent's house. My father-in-law is a fireman for the city and owns a feed and seed store, so I had to pick the right weekend to go. He was going to be on duty at the fire station on Friday night and then go directly to the store Saturday morning. He would be home Saturday night and that is when I needed to find some time to ask him for his daughter's hand in marriage. Friday night was the first step in my plan. When Leslie went upstairs to get ready for bed, I sat down with my mother-in-law, asked for her permission and then asked for her help in making sure my father-in-law and I could have some alone time to chat. She agreed to the idea of a proposal and agreed to help me get my father-in-law and me alone together.

The second part of my preparation was around how I was going to ask my father-in-law for my girlfriend's hand in marriage. I wanted to get the wording just right.

"Hey Kent, I want to marry Leslie!" No that sounded too forceful.

"Hey Kent, if you don't mind, I would like to formally ask for your blessing in the marriage of your daughter?" Nope, that sounded too formal and didn't even sound like me!

Now, I know my father-in-law well and he is not a man of many words, but I do know that when there is tension, he is always one to want to crack a joke or say something funny to lighten the load. Kent has two daughters: Leslie and Lindsey, my sister-in-law. So, in my preparation, I saw an opportunity.

"Hey Kent, is it okay if I marry your daughter?" I thought this was perfect! It was not too formal, and it gave Kent the opportunity to either say "Yes!", or to look at me and lighten the load by tilting his head and saying, "Lindsay?" Here is how I thought the conversation was going to go:

ME: "Kent, is it okay if I marry your daughter?"
KENT: "Lindsay?"
<Laughter and chuckles>
ME: "No, she is nice and all, but I meant Leslie!"
KENT: "Sure, sounds great."

Kent would then pat me on the back and make some comment about "Are you sure you want to do this?"

I rehearsed this script over and over in my head. I was prepared for him to either say yes or say Lindsay. I was convinced there was no way this was going to fail.

Do you want to guess how this went?

ME: "Hey Kent, I would like to marry your daughter." Note how I screwed this up. It was not even a question!! Even with all my practice, I screwed up the most important part of my pitch at one of the most important things I will ever do in my life.

<Before I could even correct my mistake.>

KENT: "NO!"

That was it...short and sweet...well, not so sweet, but a very short NO. I didn't get a yes; I didn't get the confused answer of Lindsay, and I did not get any laughter or chuckles. I got "NO," and then I got silence! A lot of silence.

As we sat in silence in his truck, my mind was racing. What do I do now? How do I respond? I had not practiced or prepared for "No."

Running through my head were all my possible responses. "Well your wife said yes, and we all know that her vote counts more than yours." That was probably not a good response. "Leslie told me when we get engaged, she would buy me some golf clubs as an engagement gift, so can you please say yes?" Not a good idea either. I was not prepared for No and did not have a response planned.

Finally, after what seemed like forever, (It was really only about 2 minutes), Kent went into a little speech and ultimately said that if I made her happy, then he would be happy. Then he told me to not even think about not making her happy.

While the ending of the story was good, the moral of the story is to make sure you prepare for all possible answers. For a sales rep, you need to always be prepared for "No." They will happen, even when you are feeling incredibly confident.

So, do I have you convinced to be prepared? When should you prepare? That is the next question. Many people like the saying, "Sunday, Funday!" I like Sunday Prepday. Sunday is my prep day. I will look at my week ahead and get prepared for each meeting that I have on my calendar. It may take upwards of 2 hours to get it done, but it is a great thing to do while watching your favorite TV Shows and it will prepare you for awesome weeks every time. In addition to Sunday Prepday, I review my upcoming meetings the night before to refresh my memory and to make sure nothing has changed since Sunday. If new meetings have been added to my calendar, I get ready for them as well.

One key tool you need to be prepared is a good planner. When I started my career, I bought a Franklin Covey Planner. They are not bad, but they did not work for me. I have tried electronic planners and electronic apps of all kinds, but I still prefer using paper and pen. I use a Moleskin notebook and have a page or two set aside for each meeting. I also create my own page in the journal for my daily schedule. Below is an example of a daily schedule that I use.

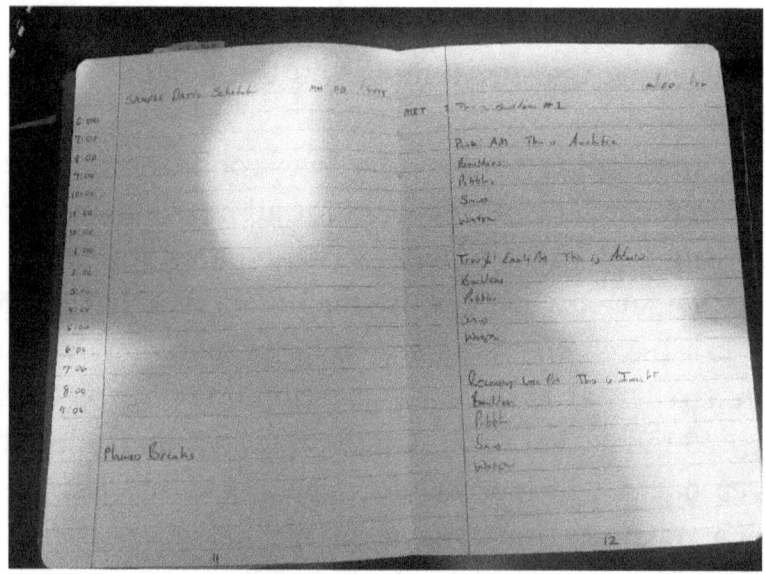

This has everything I need to get ready for a day. On the left side is my daily schedule, broken down by hour. The bottom left of the page is for my planned breaks. I try to have two breaks during the day where I plan to get away from work and do something I want. This could be a walk around the neighborhood, lunch with my wife, a simple stretch break, or time to read a book. The right side of the book is derived from another book. The title is *When* by Daniel Pink. The book's premise is that your day has three periods: Peak, Trough, and Recovery. During each part of the day, you should be doing certain tasks. I combine that thought process with the Boulder, Pebble, Sand and Water Story. This based on the story where a professor filled up a jar with large rocks all the way to the top. The professor asked the class if the jar was full. The class said it was. He then pulled out some pebbles and poured them into the jar. Pebbles fell into the jar and filled the gaps around the large rocks. Again, the professor asked the class if the jar was full. The class, not yet seeing the trend, said yes. The professor then took out some sand and poured it into the jar. The grains of sand shifted through the boulders and the pebbles to fill the gaps again. The professor again asked the class if the jar was full. Still not fully seeing the trend, the class said it was. The professor then reached for some water. The water filled all the little holes in the jar and finally the jar was full. So, I look at the boulder, pebbles, sand and water as different types of tasks. Boulders are the most important tasks that I need to complete each day. These are non-negotiables and must be done. The pebbles are important tasks, but if I do not get to them first thing today, it is not the end of the world. This could be some of the busy work we will talk about later. I must do them, but the due date is flexible. The sand represents tasks that are not that important and will not take long to finish, but I need to get them done eventually. Finally, the water represents tasks that are not that important and do not have a set deadline that I need to complete.

By first breaking my tasks into the type of tasks that fit the time of day my body is in (Peak, Trough, or Recovery) and then further qualifying them as either a Boulder, Pebble, Sand or Water allows me to be the most productive self.

Find a way to organize your day and stick with it. Make it a daily habit to create your daily and weekly plans in advance and execute that plan.

SKIP THE BUSY WORK

You can't build a reputation on what you
are going to do.
— Henry Ford

YOU NEED TO SKIP THE busy work. Every sales role in every company has busy work that you will need to complete. I am not saying that you should never do it, but rather you need to do it at the right time. For me in my current job, my clients are in the office and available from around 8 am to 6 pm, Monday through Friday. These are the prime selling hours. I spend this time calling clients, meeting with prospects, performing my discovery conversations, demonstrating our products, and closing deals. Those are all the key steps in a sales process. But those are not the only tasks you may have to complete for your job. For me I have expense reports, booking my travel, updating our Customer Relationship Management software (salesforce.com), traveling to other cities, responding to completed client satisfaction surveys and filling out forms and reports from our sales operation team. All these tasks are important and have to be done. But I often skip them. Well, I skip them during the day. I do these tasks during non-selling times. For example, when I fly, I book my travel for early in the morning or after 6pm. For me, there is a 5:15 am flight out of my local airport that will get me to American Airlines' hub in Charlotte by 6:30am. From there, I can get to just about any city in my territory before 9:00am. Worst case scenario, I am able to meet with my first client of the day by 10:00 am. When I leave a city to go home, I leave after 5:00pm. I may not get home until after 11:00pm, but at least my email is quiet, and I am not missing time to talk with my clients. I also use that time in an airplane to complete my expense report, prepare for the next day and update my Customer Relationship Management software. (When Wi-Fi is available).

The rest of my busy work gets done early in the morning or late at night. Another little tip that works for me is when you are in a hotel, use that as your late night of work. I am a husband and a father. When I am home, I want to spend time with my family. When I am in a hotel, I do not have the family responsibilities that I have when I am at home. I must take advantage of that time and work all evening, making sure I complete the busy work that I have to do. There are two reasons to push your busy work to non-selling hours. First, you want to be selling; that is why we call them selling hours! Secondly, I could easily fill up an entire day each week with busy work. I would finish my day and think, "Wow, I had a great day; I got a lot of things accomplished!" But when

I look at my activity for the day, I did not make the calls, have the meetings, or close the deals needed to keep my activity on track to help me avoid the sales roller coaster.

One time that I am willing to break this rule is when sitting on a conference call or waiting for a call to begin. For example, my current employer has a weekly sales training at 11:00 am on Monday Mornings. I will log into the meeting and it never fails, there will be roughly five to ten minutes of dead air or wasted time before the training begins. I take that time to update our Customer Relationship Software, book travel, or clean out my email. Once the training begins, I stop that and start to pay attention.

FINANCIAL PLANNING FOR A SALES PROFESSIONAL

WOULD LIKE TO PROVIDE you with a bonus chapter. This chapter is about how you should manage your finances as a sales professional. How you manage your finances will depend heavily on the type of compensation plan you have. Typically, there are three types of sales compensation plans: commission-only, salary-plus commission, and salary – plus bonus. Each one of these compensation plans has its own unique advantages and disadvantages. I will not go into which I think is best. I think the best compensation plan is the one that when combined with your product and your personal situation, allows you to help your prospects and customers while taking care of your personal financial situation. For example, a recent college grad with no spouse, no kids, and few financial obligations may be more open to a commission only job. Throughout my career, I have had each of three compensation plans.

Budgeting

Once you know the type of compensation plan and what your On-target Earnings are, you can then create your budget. On-Target Earnings, OTE, is what the company expects you to earn if you hit your goal. For example, your salary is $50,000 and if you hit your quota your commissions would be $50,000. Then your OTE is $100,000. You need to break your budget into three categories. The first category is requirements. This would be your rent, basic utilities, and food. Some of your basic utilities would be water, electricity, heat and possibly internet. Your basic food needs to be the minimum amount needed to keep you fed. That means you are not eating a steak every night, but it doesn't mean you need to have Ramen noodles every night either. The second category would be your "nice-to-haves." This could include your car (if it requires a car payment), television, extra money for clothes, and then a little more in the food budget. The third category will be your luxuries. This is for vacations, a new car or recreational items.

After you have everything in your budget separated into the different categories, it is time to see how much of your income supports your budget. If you are just getting started out in a commission only job, you need to have some savings set aside to support you during lean times. You need to be able to support your requirement items in your budget. When a big commission check comes in, you need to put some away in savings to make sure you have taken care of your budget items during a lean period. To make my example a little easier, let's look at someone getting started in a salary plus commission sales job. The salary is $35,000. That would mean that before taxes you would earn around $2,900 per month. To make my math easy, let's say your take-home pay is $2,000. You need to compare the $2,000 in take home to the amount you have in your required budget items. Your rent for an apartment you share with a few buddies runs you $500.00 per month, and your portion of electricity, gas, water and internet runs you $125.00 per month. That leaves you with an excess of $1,375. We are going to talk about debt in a few paragraphs, but let's just say that you have some student loan debt that you must pay and that equals $75.00 per month. You have determined that you can feed yourself with $300.00 per month. This means that you now have $1,000 left over for your "nice to have" budget items. You are lucky to have a functioning car that you own free and clear, so you do not need to go out and buy a new car. Your company covers your cell phone plan so that is not needed. Your "nice to have" budget items could be several things, but before you start spending that money, you need to look at your savings account. Do you have at least six months of basic living expenses in the bank? If you do, that's great. If not, then you need to start saving that extra $1,000.00 per month until you get to the six months of basic living expenses in your savings account. Then you can start using your excess to fund the "nice to have budget items." When commission checks start rolling in, you need to know a couple of things. First, they are taxed much higher than your salary so expect roughly around 50 -60% of your commissions to actually make it to your checking account. But if you are living within your budget on your salary you now have the ability to use your commission checks to support your luxury items. Maybe you want to save up and purchase a new suit, pay cash for a new car, or even make a down payment on a house. These decisions are up to you. One big caveat is if you are a commission only rep. You will want to first make sure you have 12 months of basic living expenses, then put as much in savings as possible.

Let me share with you a great example of a commission only sales professional spending his money correctly. I met Jack when I was giving him, his wife, and his daughter a tour at Elon. Jack sold large yachts down in South Florida. He was impressed with my tour of Elon and asked me if I would be interested in joining his company as a yacht broker. I went down to South Florida to meet him and the company. I was asking Jack how he handled his finances when he first got started. Here is what he told me. When he was fresh out of college, he slept on a yacht and kept the boat safe and clean for the owners in exchange for living there rent free (not a bad gig for a bachelor.) When he made his first commission on a large yacht, he put the money in his savings account and he had enough money in the bank for the next 12 months. When he made his second sale, 3 months later, he replenished his 12-month savings account and then started putting money aside to purchase a condo. After a few sales, he was able to pay cash for a one-bedroom condo in Fort Lauderdale. He lived in that condo until he met his wife. They saved up enough money and purchased a two-bedroom condo and together moved into that condo, again paying cash. They did not sell the one-bedroom condo but instead started renting it out, earning a consistent monthly income. After a few years, his wife became pregnant and they saved up enough money and this time purchased a four-bedroom condo. Again, they kept the two-bedroom as a rental. Whenever they wanted anything, they saved up and paid cash. No credit cards, no bank loans, no mortgages. His lifestyle was very modest, but because of that lifestyle, Jack was able to weather bad economic times and low commission months...or even years.

Simply put, you need to plan your budget and work your budget to make sure you can maintain a basic lifestyle. Below is a breakdown of how I would allocate my extra money each month:

- Required Budget items
- Six-month reserve = 6 x required budget items
- Nice to have budget items
- Planned purchases
- Small splurges
- Big Rewards

The key to this is to make sure you are good at budgeting when you first get started. You will get used to this lifestyle to the point that it feels normal. I now have a family of five, a mortgage payment, and dance tuition for my daughters, gymnastics tuition for my daughters as well as private school tuition. My requirement and "nice to have" budget items have expanded and become more expensive.

The reason this is so important is if you are in a tight financial situation and need to close an opportunity to make the next pay check, you will stink of desperation and people can smell desperation from a mile away. You need to not be dependent on the next sale.

Retirement

Hopefully your employer provides a 401-K, IRA, 403-B (if a non-profit) or a profit-sharing retirement plan of some type. If so, you need to contribute at least to the maximum they will match. So, if your company matches dollar for dollar up to the first six percent of your salary, you need to contribute at least six percent. I would encourage you to either talk with your company's plan provider or a friend who is a financial advisor to get an idea of how much you will need once you retire and how much you should be contributing to your retirement account.

If your company does not offer a retirement account, then you need to find a financial advisor you trust and start an IRA with them. You will not have a match from your employer, but at least you can take advantage of the tax benefits of saving for retirement.

If you are a 1099 Independent contractor, you are not going to have a retirement plan for your employer, but since you are technically running your own business, you can set up what is called a solo 401-K. I am no longer a licensed financial planner, so my advice on this type of account is to talk with your financial advisor about it and whether it can work for you.

Debt

If you cannot already tell, I am a big fan of limiting the amount of debt that you have. But I do think there is such a thing as good debt and bad debt. I would list good debt as a house, assuming it appreciates in value and a student loan, again assuming your degree can help you advance your career. Bad debt would be a car, credit card, or equity line. When you look at taking on debt, that debt needs to fit into your budget as a requirement. Can you live off your salary and meet the obligations of your debt? If the answer is yes, then I would support good debt. Go buy a house or go take some additional classes if your career could benefit from it. In most cases, I would argue bad debt is never good.

Two books I have read and liked regarding finances and debt are *The Finish Rich* Series by David Bach and *The Total Money Makeover* by Dave Ramsey. They offer in-depth advice and real-life scenarios on all the important financial topics.

Credit Cards

I would like to make a special note about credit cards concerning your business travel. When you book a hotel or rent a car and use a debit card, they will typically put a large hold on your account to cover the cost of the hotel room or the car. If you are a travelling sales rep and have a small margin between your salary and your required budget items, there may be times you are running low on funds and the hold that a hotel or rental car company puts on a debit card could wipe out your account. Because of that, I encourage you to have a credit card that you use for business travel, if you are reimbursed for those expenses. We could spend an entire chapter on which credit card is best, and that could still change frequently. I currently use a Marriott Branded Chase credit card, and I earn night credits for my Marriott Rewards account and Marriott Reward Points for my business expenses. I put all my business expenses on this card and each week, submit an expense report and when I get reimbursed, I pay off the credit card. If you are a traveling sales professional, I think this is a requirement.

Taxes

I mentioned taxes earlier and I will start this section with a disclaimer that I am not a tax expert, and I am not a Certified Public Accountant (CPA). Please consult a tax professional before doing your taxes. But you need to be aware that commissions and bonuses are taxed differently than your salary, which typically leads to higher withholdings from your commission and bonus checks. The good news, if you play your cards right, is that you should get a decent tax refund every year. The bad news, however, is that you are providing an interest free loan to the government. Being a sales professional also provides you with some additional tax benefits. If you have any expenses that you incurred that are not reimbursed by your company, you can write them off on your taxes. So, meals, travel, entertainment, supplies, car mileage and office rentals all provide you with a deduction on your taxes, assuming you can provide documentation. The key to your taxes is to be able to provide documentation for everything you claim. Maintain excellent financial records by keeping track of your miles driven and keeping all your receipts.

SALES RESOURCES

Bonus items to help you in your

sales journey

BELOW ARE SOME SALES RESOURCES that could help you as you progress in your sales journey. This is not one of the ten tips but simply some extra resources that could be helpful. I have broken the list down into podcasts, books, and other tools that could be useful for you. As of the writing of this book, none of the websites or suggestions are paying me any fee or consideration for my recommendation.

Podcasts

1. Advanced Selling Podcast (https://advancedsellingpodcast.com) Bryan Neal and Bill Caskey have been producing this Podcast for a long time. I go back and listen to several their podcasts over and over. They also have a great www.LinkedIn.com page that you can join.

2. Sell or Die Podcast (https://www.sellordieopodcast.com) Jeffery and Jennifer join forces to create a great podcast that interviews other sales people and can provide you with a wealth of quick, in-your-face information. You will find Jeffery Gitomer on several my lists.

Books

1. *The New Solution Selling* by Keith Eades. Many companies love the Solution Selling or SPI Sales Process. This book comprehensively updates the proven effective approach of Solution Selling to help you succeed with today's no-nonsense markets and buyers. A practical guide designed to provide hands-on value to frontline sales professionals as well as sales managers and executives, this step-by-step book shows you how to streamline the sales process.

2. *The Sales Bible* by Jeffery Gitomer. You are going to see him a lot. This is one of his best books. This bestselling guide to the art of the sale has helped hundreds of thousands of people get ahead in the game of sales. It offers the proven methods and techniques that lead to bigger sales and more loyal customers. Full of practical, hands-on information, it offers everything salespeople need to know to improve their results immediately.

3. *The Power to Get In* by Michael Boylan. This book is an oldie but goodie. Disregard the discussion on faxing letters and insert emailing instead. This book deals with one of the most common and frustrating problem for anyone in sales: the problem of gaining access to the

correct audience. The system provides you a step-by-step guide that will help you cut through bureaucracy, identify the people you most need to see and get in their doors.

4. *Customer Satisfaction is Worthless, Customer Loyalty is Priceless* by Jeffery Gitomer. This is the first book by Jeffery that I read, and I have since read all his books. In short, this book will teach you how to make customers love you, keep them coming back and tell everyone they know.

5. *Insight Selling* by Michael Harris. I had the opportunity to go through one of his trainings that my company did, and he was great. This book can be read in a single sitting and should get you thinking. You'll learn why insights are more likely to make it past the Buyer's defensive wall if they are hidden inside an insight scenario, like a Trojan horse. And because they transport the Buyer out of the role of a critic, and into the role of a participant, they trump verbal persuasion.

6. *The Challenger Sales Model.* I honestly have never read the full book but rather the Harvard Business Review article that discusses the book's study. If you follow solution selling, you need to read this and combine the two together.

7. *To Sell is Human* by Daniel Pink. Beside Jeffery Gitomer, Pink is one of my favorite authors. This book offers a fresh look at the art and science of selling. Pink draws on a rich trove of social science for his counterintuitive insights. He reveals the new ABCs of moving others,

explains why extraverts don't make the best salespeople, and shows how giving people an "off-ramp" for their actions can matter more than changing their minds.

8. *Predictable Revenue* by Aaron Ross. If you work for a sales startup or are responsible for building out your salesforce, this book is a great blueprint to get you started. Aaron got his start at Salesforce and helped scale their sales efforts

9. *The Sales Acceleration Formula* by Mark Roberge. This is another book that will address the science behind scaling a salesforce. If you are looking to add processes and procedures to your sales organization, this is the book for you.

10. *Authenticity: The Head, Heart and Soul of Selling* by Ron Willingham. In this book, you will go beyond the "what" to the "how" and "why" and learn whole-being selling – selling that utilizes the head, heart and soul and brings mental, emotional, and spiritual forces together.

Apps

1. Nozbe – This is my To-Do app. You can create projects for all your opportunities and create the to-dos, if you have recurring tasks, you can set those up as well.

2. Grammarly – Bad grammar can make a great presentation look like a pile of dog doo-doo. Make sure you are not making mistakes. Grammarly is not 100% accurate, but it will get you closer to better grammar.

3. LinkedIn – You need to stay in touch with your connections and keep yourself up to date; this is the best social media app for that.

4. Google Alerts – Ok, not really an app here, but I mentioned this in the preparation chapter and it is a great tool to get information delivered to your inbox about your prospects, clients and competitors.

5. Dropbox – I like to keep all my files in Dropbox to allow me to have access to all of my files across all of my electronic devices

6. DocuSign – I find that sales contracts come back faster and at all hours of the day when you send them via an electronic signature platform, and DocuSign is the most popular out there. If your company does not offer DocuSign, I encourage you to speak with your manager and get them to adopt a solution

7. MapMyCustomers – this is a mapping software that you drop pins on a map to allow you to see an overview of your territory and can help you map where to go to see prospects and clients. There are various types of mapping software out there, but this is one of the best.

Social Media Tracking

1. www.BrandYourself.com Brand Yourself can give you a scan of your Facebook, Twitter and LinkedIn profiles and look for reputation damaging posts and comments. This also looks at the first page of Google when searching your name to see if there are any damaging links

2. www.klout.com Klout gives you a score based on your social media presence, and as you improve your presence, you will see your score increase.

3. www.buffer.com The key to any online presence is to provide a value to your audience. That requires posting good information at the right times. Buffer takes care of the second piece of the puzzle. You can go into the buffer app and create content that will share across all platforms and you can schedule it to post at certain times throughout the day.

4. Analytics.twitter.com. This gives you a dashboard of information about your Twitter feed. How many tweets, impressions, profile visits, mentions and followers do you have over the last 28 days. It also looks month by month at your activity.

5. www.audiense.com Very similar to the Twitter analytics page, Audiense gives you a snapshot of your Twitter Audience

EPILOGUE

THANK YOU FOR MAKING IT to the end! I hope that you found some value within the pages of this book. I recommend that you revisit it every few months and re-read a chapter or two. If you find that you are on the sales roller coaster, re-read that chapter. Getting ready to ask someone to be a mentor? Read that chapter again. Every chapter is short enough to be read in a single sitting.

If you would like to comment on the book, please leave a rating on www.amazon.com. You can email me at bo.hamrick@bohamrick.com, tweet me at @bohamrick or connect with me on LinkedIn at www.linkedin.com/in/bohamrick. You can also check out my blog at www.bohamrick.com.

If I can be of assistance to you in any way, please feel free to reach out to me as well.

I need to thank a few more people. Thank you to Melissa Face for helping me edit this book. Your insight and assistance were immeasurable. Thank you to all my past managers for helping shape me into the sales professional that I am today. Thank you to all my clients for allowing me to serve you throughout my career. You guys are truly the reason for my success.